AYL

Litt... ...ed

Dedication

For our dear Aunty Joan, who loved all bears, especially Winnie the Pooh.

How to Make Little Needle-Felted Teddy Bears

Judy Balchin & Roz Dace

Search Press

First published in Great Britain 2014

Search Press Limited
Wellwood, North Farm Road,
Tunbridge Wells, Kent TN2 3DR

Text copyright © Judy Balchin & Roz Dace 2014

Photographs by Paul Bricknell at
Search Press Studios

Photographs and design copyright
© Search Press Ltd 2014

ISBN 978-1-78221-069-6

Suppliers
If you have difficulty in obtaining any of the
materials and equipment mentioned in this
book, then please visit the Search Press website
for details of suppliers:
www.searchpress.com

Acknowledgements
We would like to give special thanks to
Briony Dace for creating the wonderful Disco
Bear project on page 74. We would also like
to thank Moy Mackay and Gai Button for
inspiring us with their beautiful felted work.
A big thank you goes to wool suppliers
Maggie and Gary Lightfoot of Norwegian
Wool (www.norwegianwool.co.uk) for their
support. Also, David Herring of Frank Herring
and Sons (www.frankherringandsons.com) for
kindly supplying some of the wool used in
this book.
We would also like to give a huge thank you
to the Search Press team, in particular our
lovely editor Katie French for her patience and
hard work, Juan Hayward and Marrianne Miall
for their sensitive design skills, and Martin and
Caroline de la Bedoyere for loving our bears!
Finally we would like to thank all of you who
have supported us and love what we do.

Printed in China

Contents

Circus Bear 30

Baker Bear 34

Rainbow Bear 37

Vintage Bear 40

Thread Bear 43

Snow Bear 46

Wizard Bear 50

Party Bear 53

Angel Bear 56

Bride and Groom 60

Button Bear 66

Ballet Bear 70

Disco Bear 74

Arty Bear 78

Santa Paws 82

Burlesque Bear 86

Baby Bears 90

Introduction

As children we always loved making things. How fantastic now that after many years of working separately in our creative areas, we have finally merged our talents and written this book. It has been a wonderful journey and we have had a lot of fun on the way.

The discovery of wool and learning that we could sculpt almost anything from fleece, fibres and fluff, was a revelation. We couldn't wait to get started. This book is a result of a love of needle felting, which has led to us developing a sister partnership called the Woolly Felters.

Needle felting, also called dry felting, is a wonderfully simple technique. You can work round the kitchen table with friends, it does not require much room and it is inexpensive, portable and fun. All you need to start is some wool, a felting needle and a foam pad. When we started, we were excited by the creative possibilities and soon discovered that no two sculptures are exactly the same. We delighted in the quirky qualities of wool which brought a wonderful fun element into our needle-felting process.

Each of our little bears has its own appealing character. At the beginning of the book we give detailed instructions and photographs showing how to create your basic bear.

Every project offers something different and we have included many themes, from the wee woolly baby bears and Sebastian the circus bear, to Sven the snow bear and Brenda, the all singing, all dancing burlesque bear. These mini teddies do not take too long to make, they make perfect little gifts and, once you have learnt the techniques, you can create your own designs.

So, take your time, relax and enjoy the making process. We hope you will like creating your own bears and have as much fun as we have had while making our fluffy family.

Teddy Tip
All the bears in the book are between 10 and 12cm (4 and 5in) tall; the baby bears on page 90 are 7cm (2¾in) tall.

What you need

Needle felting our little bears requires only a few materials. Some wool, a felting needle and a foam pad is all you need to get started. As you progress you may want to experiment with different wools and different sized and shaped needles, but even so, this wonderful craft can be started with very little expense.

Bear necessities: wool

When starting our needle felting, we found the terminology for the different wools very confusing. After much experimentation we narrowed our choice down to two types of wool for our bears: coarser wool for the basic needle-felted bears and their clothes, and finer fibres for layering, tufting and adding details. As you become more familiar with the needle-felting process, you may want to experiment with different wools. They are all available online and from specialist outlets. Our best advice is to order a ball or two of wool and have a go!

You can see the difference clearly here between the two wools we used to create our little bears. The coarser wool is on the left and is very different from the finer Merino wool on the right.

Coarse wools for sculpting and clothing

For the basic bears and their clothes, we use coarser wools that have been washed and carded but still retain a natural crimp and spring. They are prepared as batts, which are available in dyed or naturally coloured sheets and their shorter fibres run in different directions. These batts are also available as 'slivers' or 'rovings', in which a batt has been divided into narrow lengths. They are ideal for needle-felting sculptures as they felt quickly and give a firm finish. Sometimes you will find small fragments of dried plant material in the wool. Remove these before working.

Two of the coarse wools we use are classified as mixed blends. When purchasing them, look for C1 Norwegian wool or carded 100% New Zealand wool. C1 Norwegian wool comes in a wonderful array of both vibrant and natural colours. If you are looking for a bright, modern feel, this is a good choice. It is rough and wiry and is an excellent sculpting wool with plenty of crimp. This is the first wool we worked with and we love the bright colours and its fast felting qualities.

Carded 100% New Zealand wool colours are not quite as vibrant as C1, but we love them too. This blend of wools has a wonderful dry and springy texture with lots of crimp and it is also ideal for sculpting.

We also like to use Corriedale slivers, which come from New Zealand Corriedale sheep. This wool is available in a wonderful array of colours and needle felts quickly and easily.

Finer fibres for layering, tufting and adding details

We use the finer Merino tops or combed tops for tufting and layering our bears to make them fluffy. We also use it for nose and mouth details, rosy cheeks and the finer or small decorative detailing. Coarse wool can also be used for facial and decorative detail, but its rougher quality makes it less easy to work with. The fibres in tops have been combed so that they all run in the same direction. Only the top-quality longer fibres remain after the combing process, hence the name 'tops'. The fibres feel smooth and silky and have lost the natural 'crimp' of the wool. These wools are available in a wonderful array of colours. You can purchase subtle pastel packs as well as bright, vibrant packs, or alternatively you can buy the colours singly.

Felting needles

Felting needles are made of carbon steel and have small barbs running up the blade. They are very sharp, so take care. The needles were originally designed for multiple use in industrial needle-felting machines. Used individually, wool fibres are bonded together and sculpted using a jabbing motion. The barbs on the needle blade catch the wool fibres and bind them together as you work.

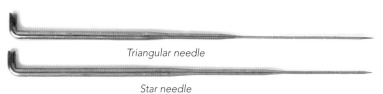

Triangular needle

Star needle

The needles we use come in different gauges with either triangular or star-shaped blades. The triangular needles are ideal for modelling basic shapes. The star needles are good for finer details and for finishing. We use triangular needles, gauge 40, for the basic bears and star needles, gauge 38, for the details and finishing.

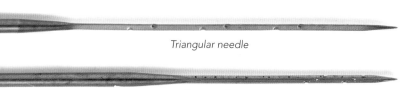

Triangular needle

Star needle

Teddy Tip
Single- and multiple-needle holders are available if you find holding the needle uncomfortable.

Foam pad

To protect yourself and your work surface from the sharp needles, you will need a foam pad to work on (see opposite). For making the bears you will need a pad measuring approximately 20cm (7¾in) square and 5cm (2in) deep. Pads can be purchased from specialist outlets or you could just buy a dense foam cushion pad from an upholsterers and cut it to size yourself. You will find that after some time the continual jabbing will cause the foam to disintegrate. When that happens, it's time to buy a new pad!

Decorative items

Adding the finishing touches to your bear's costume can really bring it to life. Add buttons, ribbons, lace, threads and anything else you can find to make your teddy extra special. We have used the following items in the projects in this book, but use anything from your crafty stash to give your bear his or her very own personality: charms, net, ribbons, buttons, lace, gems, paper flowers, embroidery threads, decorative threads, silver wire, gold wire, feathers, mini knitting needles, wool, florist's wire and shiny fibres.

Other useful things

A variety of other tools and products are useful for making needle-felted teddy bears. All can be obtained from major craft outlets and online suppliers, and many you will probably already own. These include:

I can't wait to get started!

Fondant or sugarpaste cutters: shapes can be created by needle felting wool into a fondant cutter shape.

Polystyrene (styrofoam) shapes: you can needle felt straight onto these to make all sorts of fun accessories for your bears.

Pin cushion: useful for holding pins and needles.

Small embroidery scissors: for trimming and cutting fibres.

Wooden barbecue skewer: for making shapes and accessories, such as the mini paintbrush (page 80).

Waxed dental tape: this is used for jointing the bears. We have found that the flatter dental tape works better and is stronger than dental floss.

Scalpel: for cutting slits for eye sockets.

Florist's tape: for making accessories, such as the wizard's staff (page 51).

Long needle (approximately 7cm (2¾in) long) for jointing the bears and attaching the eyes.

Sewing needle and cotton: for stitching fabrics.

Dressmaking pins: for positioning the bears' limbs before jointing and for attaching the templates to felt.

Tape measure: for measuring limbs and shapes.

Autofade pen: for drawing onto felt, such as the angel bear's wings.

Knitting needles: for hand-knitted accessories such as the snow bear's knitted hat and scarf (page 48).

Felt-tip pens: for colouring the artist bear's mini paintbrush, and for drawing designs onto polystyrene (styrofoam) shapes, such as the circus ball (page 29).

Wire cutters: for cutting lengths of florist's wire.

Dressmakers' scissors: for trimming sponge.

Teddy bear eyes: sizes 2mm and 4mm.

Glue: PVA and fabric glue.

Basic bear

The techniques for making needle-felted bears are simple. The aim is to create firm shapes using a felting needle and a bundle of wool fibres. To do this, you hold the needle upright and stab it repeatedly and deeply into the loose fibres so that the barbs on the blade bind them together firmly. It is important to needle all round the shape as you work to keep the surface even. As you needle, the shape will decrease in size by about a third.

Making your bear the right size

The basic bear measures approximately 12cm (4¾in) in height and weighs approximately 20g (¾oz). We say 'approximately' because the amounts of wool used for each bear body part may vary slightly. Enjoy the fact that no two bears can be the same!

The wool will shrink in size as you needle felt, so to help you assess how much you will need to create each body part we have provided a simple wool measuring method and finished same-size templates. We find that this is the easiest way to work out the quantities needed.

Using the basic bear templates

1 Take a handful of wool for the head and form into a ball with loose ends trailing from one side.

2 Pull the fibres tight and hold the ball next to the head template (see page 96). It should be slightly bigger than the template.

If the ball is a little small just add a layer of wool and reform it into a tight ball. If it is too big remove some wool. Continue in this way following the making instructions opposite and referring to the template whenever you are making a new body part.

This will be your technique for sizing all the body parts for the basic bear. When making the toy bear (see page 84) use the tiny bear template (see page 96). As you create more bears you will become familiar with the amounts of wool to use for each body part.

Teddy Tip

Do it like this

After needling a shape, check it is the right size against the template. If the shape is too small, add more wool and needle until smooth. If it is too big, trim it with embroidery scissors then cover the trimmed area with fibres and needle them in to create a smooth surface.

How to make a bear

Needle-felting techniques are surprisingly easy. All the body parts are needled separately and then jointed so that the limbs move. You must take care though, as the needles are sharp and barbed, so always pay attention when you are working. Here we show you how to make the basic bear. Once you know how to make this little character, you will be able to make all the bears in the book.

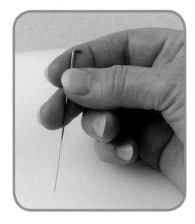

1 Using the triangular felting needle, hold the needle firmly and poke it into the fibres. Don't angle it – use a straight downwards motion, or you may find that it will break.

2 Roll the wool for the bear's head into a tight ball leaving the fibres loose on one side. Lay the ball on the foam pad and, holding the loose fibres, start to needle, turning the head round as you felt to create an even surface.

You will need

- 🐻 Coarse wool: light brown for the basic bear
- 🐻 Merino wool tops: black, pale pink
- 🐻 Triangular felting needle, gauge 40
- 🐻 Star felting needle, gauge 38
- 🐻 Foam pad
- 🐻 Wooden barbecue stick
- 🐻 Two 4mm black glass eyes with single loops
- 🐻 7cm (2¾in) needle
- 🐻 Embroidery scissors
- 🐻 Waxed dental tape
- 🐻 Scalpel

3 Keep needling until the ball shrinks to fit the template. Finish the ball and place the head to one side.

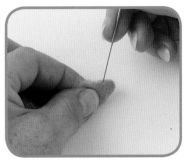

4 Take a small piece of wool for the bear's nose and needle it into a cone shape, leaving loose fibres trailing from the base of the cone. Put to one side.

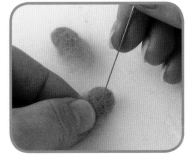

5 Felt two small semi-circles for the ears, leaving the flat edges unfelted. Again, put to one side.

Teddy Tip

When making ears, arms and legs, you may find it easier to measure out two equal amounts of wool for each pair before you start needling.

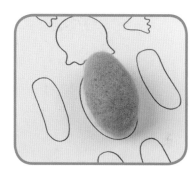

6 Roll a tight oval for the body between your fingers and needle it, turning it as you work to achieve an even finish.

7 Complete one rounded end, then work down the oval and needle all the loose fibres to create a smooth shape. Match the size of the finished body with the template.

8 Place the bear's head onto the top of the oval body, spreading the loose fibres over the shoulders. Needle them firmly to secure the head.

Teddy Tips
Angling the bear's head slightly when securing it to the body can give a more appealing look.

Ears can be shaped once they are secured. Needle into their centres to angle them inwards.

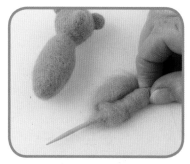

9 Lay the base of the nose cone onto the front of the head so that the loose fibres splay out. Needle the loose fibres into the head.

10 Attach an ear to either side of the head by needling the loose fibres into the head.

11 To create the first arm, wrap wool tightly round the end of a barbecue stick to make a sausage shape.

12 Slip the wool off the stick and needle it in the middle to secure the sausage shape.

13 Needle the end of the sausage shape to make it round.

14 Work down the shape, needling it to make it firm. When the arm is the same length as the template, round off the other end. Repeat for the second arm.

15 Create a slightly thicker sausage shape for the leg using the same technique. Press one end of the shape onto your foam pad so that the foot bends slightly and then needle the inner fold firmly. Repeat for the second leg.

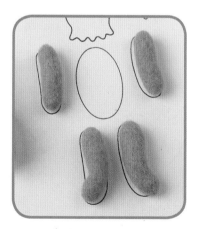

16 Place the arms and legs on the template to make sure they are the same size. If necessary, add wool to the shapes, or trim away excess fibres with embroidery scissors. Work over cut areas with the needle and some fibres to smooth the surfaces.

17 When you have completed the body parts use a star needle to work over each of the shapes. Needle in any stray fibres to give a smooth finish. You will not have to do this if you are going to tuft or layer your bear.

Teddy Tip
While working, you can roll any shape in your hands to help the binding process.

Will you play with me?

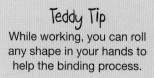

Check that both arms and both legs are the same length. If they're not, trim the longer one to the right size using embroidery scissors.

Making faces

Adding the features is like waving a magic wand to bring your little bear to life and introduce you to his or her unique character.

Attaching the eyes

When the first teddy bears were made, shoe buttons were mainly used for their eyes. Nowadays, glass eyes are specially manufactured in a huge range of sizes and colours. For our teddies, we have used either 2mm or 4mm black glass eyes with a single loop. Beads are an inexpensive alternative and are threaded in the same way as the glass eyes. Eyes with wire loops are available from specific online teddy bear product suppliers. They are attached to the bear with waxed dental tape as this is extremely strong and durable. You will need a long needle to attach the eyes.

1 Create the eye sockets by repeatedly stabbing the needle into the head to create two indented circles above the nose.

2 Use the tip of a scalpel to make a small slit in the centre of each socket.

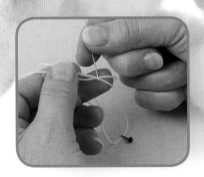

3 Thread a 20cm (7¾in) length of dental tape through the loop of the first eye. Put the two tape ends together and thread them onto a long needle.

4 Push the needle through the slit and out through the base of the back of the head. Pull the eye tight into the socket and leave the ends trailing.

5 Repeat steps 3 and 4 for the second eye with a separate length of dental tape.

6 Make sure that the thread emerges from the back of the head adjacent to the first threads.

7 Tie the ends of the tape together in a secure knot.

8 Thread them one at a time through the body.

9 Trim the ends of the tape close to the body.

Adding the nose, mouth and rosy cheeks

1 Using a thin strand of black Merino wool, needle a triangular outline onto your bear's nose.

2 Needle the centre of the nose with more wool.

3 Needle another thin length of wool to the base of the nose. Take it a little way down below the nose and then needle it into the face to secure it.

4 Divide this strand in two, pull the two strands apart and needle one to each side of the face to create the mouth. Trim the ends to neaten.

5 If you want your bear to have rosy cheeks, needle a few strands of pink Merino wool into the cheek area to create a gentle rosy glow.

6 Trim off the excess fibres close to the bear's face. Needle any loose fibres on the head with the star needle to neaten.

Bringing your bear to life

Creating your teddy's face is important, as it will dictate the nature and characteristics of your bear. Varying the size of nose cones, nose details, eyes and ears will give different looks and characters. Also, where you place the features will have a dramatic effect, conveying a whole range of emotions: happy, sad, cuddly, naughty, thoughtful or surprised. A huge range of expressions can be captured easily, as shown here.

Noses

Nose cones can be small or large, long and pointed or short and squashed. They can be placed in the centre or on the lower half of the head. A bear's nose is particularly important and can make a huge difference to the look of your bear.

Large squashed nose cone on the lower part of the face, and a large nose.

Small elongated nose cone on the lower part of the face, and a small nose.

Small nose cone in the centre of the face, and a small nose.

Medium nose cone on the lower part of the face, and a medium nose.

Eyes and ears

We have used two different sized eyes in this book. The size of the eyes and where they are placed on the bear's face is of the utmost importance. Once the eyes are in place your bear will come alive! Ears, too, have a huge effect on the look of your bear. Their size, shape and positioning will give you plenty of opportunity to stuff your little teddy bear full of character.

Small ears on the top of the head; small eyes close together and a medium nose.

Small ears on the side of the head; large eyes wide apart and a small nose.

Medium ears spaced apart; small eyes spaced apart and a medium nose.

Big ears on the top of the head; big eyes close together and a medium nose.

Colourful bears

Colour also plays a big part in conveying the character of your bear, whether it be pastel or bright, traditional or fun. You can use just a few contrasting colours, or really go to town with a multi-coloured teddy. It's a bit like painting with wool!

Pastel pink head; contrasting bright pink nose and mouth details.

Bright turquoise head; contrasting paler turquoise nose cone and ears.

Orange head; yellow nose cone with red nose and mouth details; touches of red to add depth to the eyes and ears.

A gloriously multi-coloured and vibrant bear who isn't afraid to embrace colour!

Paws and feet

Our basic bear has very simple paws, legs and feet. Essentially, each paw and foot is made by needling a sausage shape. Sometimes, however, our bears demand paws with thumbs or bigger feet with toes, perhaps flat feet so that they can stand or even boots for the colder weather. We like to keep them happy!

Feet with toes

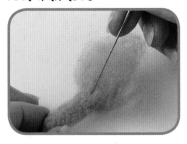

1 Use a wooden barbecue stick to shape a sausage of wool, as for a basic leg. Needle the sausage firmly down to the ankle, leaving loose fibres at the end.

2 Stand the sausage upright on your foam pad with the loose fibres splayed at the bottom.

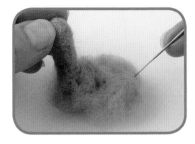

3 Add more wool for the foot and needle round the edge of the foot with the needle angled towards the centre.

4 Needle the whole of the upper foot until the wool starts to bind together and shrink to a flattened oval shape.

5 Turn the foot over and place it so that the leg hangs down the side of the foam pad. Needle the sole of the foot.

6 Continue needling the top, edge and bottom of the foot until you are satisfied with the foot shape. Repeatedly needle two indented lines into the foot to create the three toes.

Standing feet

If you would like your bear to stand up, follow steps 1–3 for making feet with toes above, but make the sausage shapes slightly thicker, as these legs will be supporting your bear when it is standing. Then follow steps 1 and 2 here.

1 Add some wool for the foot, but this time needle it into a shoe shape.

2 Needle the bottom of the shoe flat.

Bears with boots

Follow the instructions for the standing feet on page 20, then follow the steps below.

1 Wrap each foot and ankle with coloured coarse wool. Starting at the ankle, work your way down and along the foot, needling until the coloured wool is firm and secure.

2 Roll some contrasting coarse wool between the palms of your hands to create a warm woolly cuff for your bear's boot.

3 Needle the cosy trim round the top of the boot – perfect for cold weather bears.

Paws with thumbs

Now and again our teddy friends want to hold something in their paws, so we have helped them by making flattened paws with thumbs. Whether it be a paintbrush, a snowball, a balloon or even a magic staff, the larger paws are very popular with the bears.

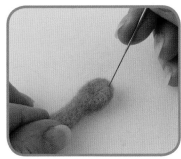

1 Needle a sausage arm as for the basic bear, leaving loose fibres at one end.

2 Lay the sausage flat on the foam pad with the loose ends trailing and add a ball of wool. Needle it to a flat disc shape.

3 Needle a small sausage on your foam pad for the thumb leaving loose fibres at one end, and then needle it to the side of the disc.

Making furry bears

We realise that a lot of bear owners have loved the fur off their bears, but some teddies do feel the cold, so a few of our bears are fluffy, and the following two techniques are for them. Both are applied before jointing the bear.

We use Merino tops to make our bears fluffy. It is available in many different colours and is beautifully soft. We have used one colour for the layering technique, and we have mixed colours when tufting. Make sure that the basic bear is needle felted very firmly. If it is not, the tufting and layering will not be secure.

Layering

Layering gives a smoother furry look than tufting, and fibres are layered up and round the bear in the same way as fur would grow naturally, then trimmed back to resemble teddy fur.

Bare layered bear

Finished layered bear

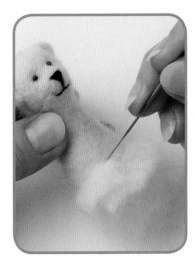

1 Cut a 2cm (¾in) wide strip across the Merino fibres.

2 Fold the fibres in half lengthways, then lay them down from the bottom of the bear up in the direction that the fur would grow, and needle a line firmly over the fold.

3 Work upwards to the neck with the strips needled on in lines, strip over strip. When layering fibres over the face, they should radiate outwards from the eyes and nose, as the fur would grow naturally.

4 Trim the fibres to a short length using a small pair of embroidery scissors as you finish each body part.

5 Layer the fibres on the arms and legs in the same way.

6 Needle the trimmed fibres into all the body parts, enough to retain the 'furry' look, then joint your bear (see pages 26–27).

Tufting

Tufting gives your bear a much loved though slightly tatty look, with small tufts of wool needled in all over the bear, apart from on the nose cone, paws and feet.

Bare tufted bear

Finished tufted bear

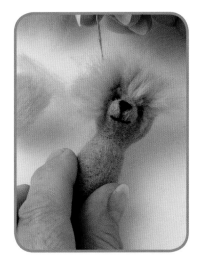

1 Cut a 2cm (¾in) wide strip across the blue Merino fibres. Work round each eye with small tufts of wool, needling them so that they radiate outwards like sun rays. Needle the centre of the strip into the bear so that the fibres stand up.

2 Leaving the nose cone and ears untufted, continue adding tufts of grey wool over the head and body.

3 Trim the fibres back to approximately 3mm (⅛in) long.

4 Tuft the arms and legs, leaving the paws and feet untufted.

The tufted bear, jointed and ready to go!

Jointing the bears

Durable waxed dental tape is used for jointing the bears. You will also need a 7cm (2¾in) needle. It should be long enough to go through one leg, the body and the second leg, leaving enough of the needle protruding so that you can hold it.

Lay the bear in front of you with the legs and body in the right positions. You can pin the limbs to the body to get the positioning right before jointing. Remove the pins when you are happy with the look of your bear, before you start the jointing process. The jointing technique is the same for the legs as it is for the arms.

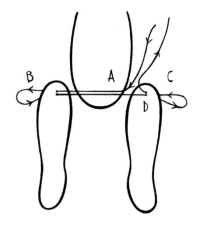

1 Thread the needle with approximately 40cm (16in) of dental tape. Push it in at point A, through the body and out the other side.

2 Pass the needle through the top of the bear's right leg. Pull the thread through at point B, leaving approximately 10cm (4in) hanging from point A.

3 Pass the needle back through the leg and into the body, as close as possible to where it came out.

4 Push the needle through the body and the bear's left leg at C. Make sure the legs are symmetrical.

Teddy Tip

When you have completed your basic bear, give teddy a close shave and trim any loose fibres with embroidery scissors.

Ooh! It tickles!

5 Pull the thread through, then pass the needle back through the leg adjacent to the thread at point D.

6 Pull the thread tightly so that the bear's limbs are firmly jointed. Tie the ends of tape together in a knot.

7 Thread the ends one by one back into the bear's body and trim away the excess tape.

8 Hide the holes where the tape passed through. See the Teddy Tip below.

Teddy Tip
Cover any stitches or holes you've made when jointing or sewing on buttons by needling over them using a tiny piece of matching wool.

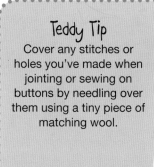

Will it hurt?

Extra bear bits

Throughout the book we create flat needle-felted panels for making the bears' costumes and accessories. Using the technique below you can make many things, including, as we show in this book, a wedding dress, a ballet tutu, a skirt, an artist's palette and a chef's hat.

Needling a flat piece

When you needle felt a bear, the fibres shrink as they bind together. The same shrinking process happens when creating a flat panel, but you have to angle the needle to help the process along, as shown in step 4.

To create a flat felted panel for clothing, follow the instructions below. If you require a more substantial flat shape such as Arty Bear's paint palette (see page 80), simply follow the same technique but keep needling the panel until it shrinks further to become thicker and firmer.

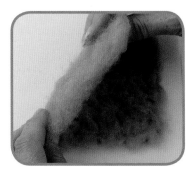

1 Lay the coarse wool on your foam pad. Lay a paper template of the required finished panel on top, and make sure the wool covers an area approximately one third larger than the template.

2 Needle the wool evenly all over, holding the needle at right angles to the foam pad, until the fibres start to bind together.

3 Gently pull the wool away from the foam pad and turn it over.

4 Holding the needle so that it is angled towards the centre of the panel, needle shallowly across the fibres. This will start to shrink the panel to the required size.

5 Continue in this way, needling at an angle and turning the panel frequently until it has shrunk to slightly larger than the template. Turn it and needle it once more holding the needle upright. You should have achieved a firm, even panel. If there are any thin areas that you can see through, simply add some more wool and needle until even.

6 Pin your template to the panel and cut round it. Needle round the edge of the panel to neaten if necessary.

Using a cookie or fondant cutter

You can create simple, three-dimensional felted shapes using metal or plastic cookie cutters or fondant cutters. It does take time to needle the final shape smooth, but the results are well worth it!

1 Press your cutter firmly onto your foam pad. Load it with wool and then needle the fibres until they shrink down into the cutter and bind together. Make sure you needle firmly round the inner edge of the cutter.

2 When the fibres are firm, remove the cutter and gently peel the shape away from the foam pad.

3 Needle the shape to bind the fluffy fibres. Turn it frequently and continue needling until you achieve a smooth, firm shape.

Covering a polystyrene (styrofoam) shape

A polystyrene (styrofoam) shape makes an ideal core for needle felting. You can successfully needle felt different colours onto your polystyrene surface to create an attractive design.

1 First draw your design onto the polystyrene shape with a felt-tip pen.

2 Lay the coloured fibres over the section you want to work on and needle them into the polystyrene, filling each part.

The finished ball.

Circus Bear

Let the show begin and the bears perform. Here comes Sebastian, tumbling his way onto the page with his colourful balancing ball. Dressed in his jaunty hat and colourful ruff, he is ready to fall head over heels just for you!

You will need

* Coarse wool: light grey for the bear; red, yellow, jade and orange for the hat, nose, pompoms, shoes and ball
* Merino tops: black and pink for mouth details and rosy cheeks
* Two 2mm black glass eyes with a single loop
* 4cm (1½in) wide wired organza ribbon in orange, 25cm (10in) long
* Orange thread
* 7cm (2¾in) diameter polystyrene (styrofoam) ball

Tools

* Triangular felting needle, gauge 40
* Star felting needle, gauge 38
* Foam pad
* Embroidery scissors
* Dressmaking pins
* Waxed dental tape
* Long needle
* Wooden barbecue stick
* Sewing needle
* Felt-tip pen
* Fabric glue

Instructions

1 Create the bear's head, nose cone, ears, body, arms and legs using light grey coarse wool by following the instructions on pages 12–17. Needle the head to the body, then needle the nose cone to the head and attach the ears so that they sit low on each side of the head. Attach the eyes. Needle the mouth in black Merino wool, then needle a little pink Merino wool into each cheek and trim back. Joint your bear as shown on pages 26–27.

Diagram for ball design

2 Wrap a foot in jade wool. Holding the wool tight to the foot, needle it to secure the fibres and create the shoe. Repeat for the other foot.

3 To make the hat, first use a barbecue stick to roll a 6cm (2¼in) long sausage of jade wool.

4 Slip the stick out of the wool. Needle one end of the sausage to a point. Needle and shape the other end to make a cone that will sit comfortably between the bear's ears.

5 Roll a sausage of orange wool between your hands, wrap it round the bottom of the cone hat and needle it to secure.

6 Holding the cone upside down on your foam pad, repeatedly needle the inside of the flat end to make it concave so that it sits comfortably on the bear's head.

7 Spread a little glue onto the bottom of the cone, press it onto the bear's head and then needle round the edge of the cone.

8 Make three jade balls, three orange and one small red one. To create each ball, take a small piece of wool, lay it on your foam pad and stab it with your needle as you move it round so that it forms a loose ball.

9 Wet your hands slightly and then roll the ball between your palms and fingers. The ball will become smaller and tighter. Repeat the stabbing and rolling process a few times until the ball is firm.

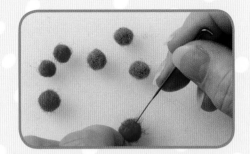

10 Needle one orange ball to the top of the cone hat and one to each shoe.

11 Needle three jade balls down the bear's chest and the small red ball to the bear's nose.

12 To create the ruff, fold the ribbon down its length. Leaving a 10cm (4in) length of thread, sew a row of small running stitches along the ribbon just below the fold.

13 Gather the ribbon so that it fits comfortably round the bear's neck and then tie the two thread ends in a knot. Trim the ends.

14 Using the diagram to help you, draw the star pattern onto either end of a polystyrene ball. Draw two parallel lines round the middle of the ball and then add vertical lines running from the points of the star to the centre lines.

15 Needle different coloured wools into the ball as shown on page 29.

Baker Bear

Billy has been busy baking tasty cakes and is looking forward to the teddy bear's picnic with his friends. He has a round tummy, his nose is small, and his ears are attached low on the sides of this head, allowing room for his chef's hat.

You will need

* Coarse wool: brown for the bear; white, beige, pink and red for the chef's hat and cake
* Merino tops: black and red for the nose, cheeks and mouth
* Two 2mm black glass eyes with a single loop
* Narrow satin ribbon: pink, 20cm (7¾in) long

Tools

* Triangular felting needle, gauge 40
* Star felting needle, gauge 38
* Foam pad
* Small foam block for forming chef's hat
* Embroidery scissors
* Scissors
* Dressmaking pins
* Waxed dental tape
* Wooden barbecue stick
* Long needle
* Fabric glue

Template for Billy's hat, half size

Instructions

1 Make the basic bear (see pages 12–17), adding more fibres round the lower body to create a fat tummy. Attach the head to the body. Add the ears and eyes, then needle the features, adding a few red Merino fibres to each cheek. Joint the bear following the instructions on pages 26–27.

Teddy Tip
Instructions for making the cakes, loaves and cookies can be found on pages 92 and 93.

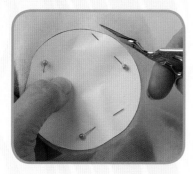

2 Use coarse wool to create the chef's hat. Referring to page 28, create a flat felt band and circle. Using the templates provided opposite, cut the band and the circle to the correct size.

3 Cut a cylinder out of the small foam block and trim it to measure 5cm (2in) long, with a diameter of 3cm (1¼in).

4 Lay the felt circle on top of the cylinder and bring the edges down. Gather and gently needle them into the foam base. Wrap the hat band round the bottom of the gathered hat and needle it to secure.

5 Gently pull the finished hat away from the foam.

6 Position the hat on the bear's head and needle it securely all round. Tie a ribbon round the bear's neck and trim the ends.

7 Make the cake (see page 92) and glue it between the bear's paws. Secure further with needling if necessary.

Rainbow Bear

A bear's aim in life is to be cuddled and hugged as much as possible. With her soft rainbow coat of fluffiness, Rosie is certain to get more hugs than most! We use a needle-felted flower with a ribbon bow to create a mini hairband for our furry friend. To give Rosie a cute look, needle a slightly wider, squashed nose cone and attach the ears low down on the side of her head.

You will need

* Coarse wool: white for the bear
* Merino tops: white, lemon, pale pink, pale green and lilac for tufting and features
* Two 4mm black glass eyes with a single loop
* 2mm wide satin ribbon: pale green, 20cm (7¾in) long

Tools

* Triangular felting needle, gauge 40
* Foam pad
* Embroidery scissors
* Dressmaking pins
* Waxed dental tape
* Long needle
* Wooden barbecue stick
* Fabric glue

Instructions

1 Using white coarse wool and referring to pages 12–17, first make your bear's head, nose cone, ears, body, arms and legs. Make the large feet and toes, as shown on page 20. Needle the head to the body, then attach the nose cone, ears and eyes to the head. Add the nose and mouth details in lilac Merino wool.

2 Using the tufting guide on page 25 to help you, tuft the bear. First work round each eye with small tufts of lilac fibres, needling them so that they radiate outwards like sun rays.

3 Now tuft the bear's head and body with different coloured wools, and tuft the chest with white wool. Leave the nose cone and ears untufted. Every now and again, trim the fibres back to give the fluffy look.

4 Tuft the bear's arms and legs in the same way, leaving the paws and feet untufted. Needle a small lilac circle to each toe and a larger one to create the footpad. Needle a small lilac circle on to the inside of each paw.

5 Joint the arms and legs to the body using the jointing technique shown on pages 26–27.

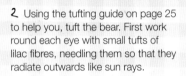

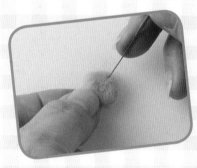

6 To make the decorative flower lay a small ball of lilac fibres on to the foam pad and needle it. Turn it over and needle it further until it is a flat disc of matted fibres approximately 1cm (½in) across.

7 Needle a few strands of lemon coloured fibres into the centre of the disc.

8 Glue, or sew, a length of ribbon around the bear's head and add a ribbon bow near the ear.

9 Attach the disc to the ribbon with a spot of glue. Needle round the edge to secure it.

Vintage Bear

Victoria loves vintage lace and ribbons. She is an old-fashioned bear and you can sometimes find her in the Honeyhills market looking for bargains. Early teddy bears often had longer noses, so Victoria's nose is lengthened a little and she is wearing a beautiful vintage lace dress, with a rose in one furry ear.

You will need

* Coarse wool: pale beige for the bear
* Merino tops: light brown and black for layering and for the nose and mouth details
* Two 2mm black glass eyes with a single loop
* Ivory lace, 11 x 7cm (4¼ x 2¾in)
* Narrow satin pink ribbon: 45cm (17¾in) long
* White sewing thread
* Miniature paper flowers

Tools

* Triangular felting needle, gauge 40
* Foam pad
* Wooden barbecue stick
* Embroidery scissors
* Scissors
* Dressmaking pins
* Waxed dental tape
* Sewing needle
* Long needle
* Fabric glue

Instructions

1 Referring to pages 12–20, needle the bear's head using pale beige coarse wool, then needle the nose cone, elongating it slightly. Needle the ears, the body, the arms and the legs with standing feet. Attach the head to the body, and the nose cone, ears and eyes to the head. Add the nose and mouth details.

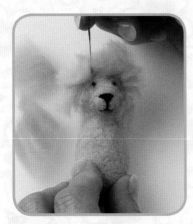

2 Using the layering guide on page 23 to help you, and light brown Merino wool, layer the bear, adding layers of fibres to the body, head, arms and legs. After layering, trim the fur and tousle it by rubbing it gently with your fingers to give it an aged look.

3 Joint the legs, following the instructions on pages 26–27.

4 To dress vintage bear, cut enough lace to wrap round her, with an overlap. Stitch the lace to the bear, then sew up the back seam.

5 Tie a length of pink ribbon round the top of the lace, and finish it off with a bow at the front.

6 Joint the arms, following the instructions on pages 26–27, and then glue a bunch of miniature flowers to the bear's paw. Glue a single flower to her ear.

Thread Bear

Theodora Thread Bear has literally been loved to bits. She
has lost half an ear and both eyes. Her body is saggy, baggy,
patched and tired, but she is, and has been, well loved, and
that is what bears are for!

You will need

* Coarse wool: light brown for the bear; pale yellow,
  rust and dark brown for the patches, hairband and
  paw pads
* Merino tops: dark brown for the nose and mouth details
* Small orange button
* Brown embroidery thread

Tools

* Triangular felting needle, gauge 40
* Star felting needle, gauge 38
* Foam pad
* Wooden barbecue stick
* Embroidery scissors
* Dressmaking pins
* Waxed dental tape
* Long needle
* Sewing needle

Instructions

1 Using light brown coarse wool and referring to pages 12–17, make your bear's head, nose cone, one complete ear, one half ear, and arms. Make the legs with big feet and toes as described on page 20.

2 Needle one rounded end of your oval for the body. Holding this rounded end, needle the loose fibres until the body takes on a bent, slightly slumped and flattened appearance.

3 Attach the head to the body, and the nose cone and the one and a half ears to the head. Add the nose and mouth details with dark brown Merino wool.

4 Needle a few dark brown strands into and round one eye socket. Sew a button into this eye socket and stitch a cross over the other socket using brown embroidery thread.

5 Joint your bear loosely so that the limbs are slightly floppy. See pages 26–27.

6 On the bottom of each foot, needle three small brown circles and a larger one for the pad.

7 To create the patches, needle small squares of pale yellow and rust wool randomly over your bear.

8 Sew round each patch with brown thread using small stitches.

9 Needle a length of rust coloured wool round the head to create a headband.

10 Add a few tufts of pale yellow wool near the ear.

Snow Bear

Sven bear loves to play in the snow. His winter white coat is layered on and he has a warm knitted blue hat and scarf to keep out the winter chills. His snug boots are needled on over his teddy legs and they are fashionably trimmed with fluffy wool. To make Sven's two little friends, shown on page 49, just needle the basic bear parts smaller than the template.

You will need

* Coarse wool: white for bear, bobble, snowball and fur trim; beige for boots
* Merino tops: white and black for layering, and nose and mouth details
* Two 2mm black glass eyes with a single loop
* 4-ply (fingering) yarn in blue
* Sewing thread

Tools

* Triangular felting needle, gauge 40
* Foam pad
* Wooden barbecue stick
* Embroidery scissors
* Dressmaking pins
* Waxed dental tape
* Long needle
* Knitting needles, 2.5mm (US size 1)
* Tapestry needle

Instructions

1 Using white coarse wool and referring to pages 12–20, make the bear's head, nose cone and two ears, arms with thumbs, standing legs and body. Attach the head to the body. Attach the nose cone, and then the two ears low down on the head to allow room for the hat. Attach the eyes, and add the nose and mouth details with black Merino wool.

2 Using white Merino wool, layer the fibres over the unjointed bear parts, using the layering technique on page 23.

3 Using the beige coarse wool, wrap lengths of fibre round one leg and foot, and needle them firmly in place, shaping the front of the boot so it is smooth and round. Keep adding the fibres until the boot is complete. Repeat on the other leg.

4 Roll a length of coarse white wool between your palms and wrap it round the top of each boot to hide any untidy fibres. Needle to secure.

5 Joint the bear, following the instructions on pages 26–27. Using white coarse wool, needle a small smooth, round snowball. Place the bear's left paw on the foam pad and needle the ball firmly into his palm.

6 Make a white bobble for his hat in the same way.

7 Knit the bear's hat and scarf following the instructions on page 48. Sew the bobble to the top of the hat, and sew the hat to his head. Tie the scarf round his neck.

Knitted hat

Cast on 30 stitches, then knit 2 rows and purl 1 row.

Work next 2 rows in stocking (stockinette) stitch, starting with a knit row.

Continue in stocking (stockinette) stitch, decreasing on the knit rows as follows:

Row 1: K4, K2tog, K8, K2tog, K8, K2tog, K4 (27 sts).

Row 3: K4, K2tog, K7, K2tog, K7, K2tog, K3 (24 sts).

Row 5: K4, K2tog, K6, K2tog, K6, K2tog, K2 (21 sts).

Row 7: K4, K2tog, , K5, K2tog, K5, K2tog, K1 (18 sts).

Row 9: K4, K2tog, K4, K2tog, K4, K2tog (15 sts).

Row 11: K4, K2tog, K3, K2tog, K4 (12 sts).

Row 12: Purl.

Cut the yarn to a 30cm (11¾in) length. Thread it onto a needle and then through the remaining 12 stitches. Pull tight.

To make up

Use the long end and the tapestry needle to sew the two hat seams together, working any ends in neatly.

Knitted scarf

Cast on 4 stitches and knit 67 rows in stocking (stockinette) stitch. Cast off.

Snow teddy

You will need:

* Coarse wool: white, orange and black
* Two twigs
* Two 4mm beads for the eyes
* Sewing needle
* White thread

1 Use white wool to loosely needle felt a fluffy, soft 6cm (2¼in) ball for the body.

2 In the same way, needle felt a 4cm (1½in) diameter ball for the head.

3 Needle two semicircles for the ears and needle them onto the head.

4 Needle a small cone for the carrot nose using orange wool. Attach the nose.

5 Attach the eyes using the instructions on pages 16 and 17 to help you. Then needle the mouth and the black spots on the body.

6 Use a scalpel to cut a slit on either side of the body.

7 Push a twig into each of the slits and then needle round the twig to firm the fibres.

Wizard Bear

Dylan is the wisest and oldest bear. He loves travelling, reading books, casting spells and looking after all the other bears. He is made in the same way as his friends, but is magically transformed with the addition of a tall wizard's hat, little pointed boots, beads and charms.

You will need

* Coarse wool: turquoise for the bear; dark red, yellow and white for the hat, boots, star and staff
* Merino tops: black for the nose and mouth
* Two 2mm black glass eyes with a single loop
* Crystal bead
* Two key charms
* Seed bead for the earring
* Short length of metallic thread for the necklace
* Sewing thread
* Florist's wire, 10cm (4in) long, florist's tape, gold wire and two different-sized beads for the staff

Tools

* Triangular felting needle, gauge 40
* Star felting needle, gauge 38
* Foam pad
* Small star-shaped cookie or fondant cutter
* Wooden barbecue stick
* Embroidery scissors
* Dressmaking pins
* Waxed dental tape
* Long needle
* Sewing needle
* Fabric glue

Instructions

1 Using turquoise coarse wool and referring to the instructions on pages 12–17, make the bear's head, nose cone, ears and body. Needle the head to the body. Needle the nose cone to the head and attach the ears, low down on the sides of the head to allow room for the hat, then attach the eyes. Needle the nose and mouth details. Sew a seed bead onto one ear.

2 Needle two arms with flattened paws and thumbs, as shown on page 21. Bend one arm at the elbow by needling repeatedly into the inside of the arm in the fold. Glue a crystal bead onto the palm.

3 Needle two legs with standing feet, following the instructions on page 20.

4 Make the boots using the coarse red wool. Wrap lengths of fibre round one foot and ankle and needle them firmly in place, shaping the front of the boot so that it is smooth and pointed. Keep adding the fibres until the boot is complete. Repeat on the other leg. Now joint your bear as shown on pages 26–27.

5 To make the hat, needle a flat-bottomed cone, leaving a length of loose fibres at the top. The base of the cone should sit neatly on the bear's head. Needle the loose fibres into a long sausage shape to form the top of the hat.

6 Fold the end of the sausage over then, where the fold falls, needle into the underside to curl the end of the hat.

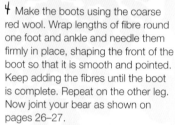

7 Needle a flat circle, 7cm (2¾in) diameter, for the rim of the hat as shown on page 28, then needle the cone to the centre of the circle. Needle into the hat base to made it concave so that it fits snugly on the bear's head. Attach the hat to the head firmly, needling it all round.

8 Using the small star-shaped cutter, needle felt the star as shown on page 29. Sew the star to the end of the hat.

9 Thread two key charms onto a short length of metallic thread and tie them loosely round the bear's neck.

10 To make the staff, wrap a 12cm (4¾in) length of florist's wire first with florist's tape, then with white coarse wool. Spiral gold wire along the length of the staff, then glue the larger of the two beads to the top, followed by the smaller bead.

Party Bear

Oh dear, Polly has so many balloons that she is floating up into the clouds! Here she is all dressed up in her new dress and matching hair bow. Let's hope her teddy friends will be able to help her down so that she can enjoy a slice of her birthday cake.

You will need

* Coarse wool: light brown for the bear; pale blue, white, light pink, dark pink, turquoise, lemon and pale green for the party dress, hair bow and balloons
* Merino tops: black for the nose and mouth
* Two 4mm black glass eyes with a single loop
* Five 10cm (4in) lengths of florist's wire
* Thin wire, 10cm (4in) long

Tools

* Triangular felting needle, gauge 40
* Star felting needle, gauge 38
* Foam pad
* Wooden barbecue stick
* Embroidery scissors
* Dressmaking pins
* Waxed dental tape
* Long needle
* Fabric glue
* Bull-nose plyers

Instructions

1 Referring to pages 12–21, use light brown coarse wool to make your bear's head, nose cone, ears, body, arms with hands and thumbs, and legs with standing feet. Attach the head to the body, then needle the nose cone and ears to the head. Attach the eyes then needle the nose and smiling mouth.

2 Wrap the top of each arm with pale blue wool and needle until firm to create the sleeves.

3 Needle a border of white wool round the bottom of each sleeve.

Teddy Tip

To create the spots on the dress, twirl the fibres round the shaft of your needle as you needle. This will give you more control of the fibres as they felt.

4 Wrap the body with pale blue wool and needle it until it is smooth and secure.

5 Use thin strands of white wool to needle a border round the neck of the dress.

6 Needle small circles of white wool evenly over the bodice of the dress to create the polka dot pattern.

7 To make the skirt, refer to page 28 and layer a 5 x 25cm (2 x 9¾in) area of pale blue wool on your foam pad and needle it until it shrinks to approximately 3.5 x 17cm (1½ x 6¾in). Trim it to neaten the edges.

8 Starting at the back of the bear, needle the long edge into her waist. Gather the strip as you needle it round the bear to give the skirt a full look. Slightly overlap the join at the back of the skirt and loosely needle it together. Joint the bear (see pages 26–27).

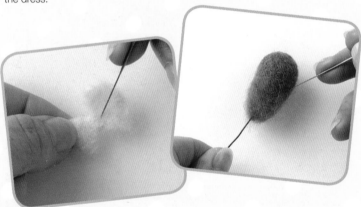

9 To make the hair bow, lay a 2 x 3cm (¾ x 1¼in) area of white wool on your foam pad and needle it flat until it shrinks to 1 x 2cm (½ x ¾in).

10 Needle the centre of the strip to create the bow shape and then continue needling into the edges of the bow to neaten.

11 Needle the bow to the bear's head.

12 To make the balloons, fold over the end 1cm (½in) of one length of florist's wire and place the folded end in the centre of a ball of coloured wool.

13 Needle the wool into an oval shape. The wire will be running down the middle of the balloon, so be gentle when needling this area.

14 Needle the end of the oval where the wire protrudes slightly more so that it shrinks to create a balloon shape.

15 Make four balloons in the same way using different coloured wools and then lay the balloon wires together and wrap them with a thin piece of wire.

16 Lay the wires across the bear's paw. Add a blob of glue, close the paw and pin the closed paw to the foam pad with a felting needle until the glue has set hard.

Angel Bear

Alice, our ethereal Angel Bear, floats silently on her woolly cloud. Her tufts are soft, and her dress is a swirling fan of flowing fibres. It is Alice's task to look after all the bears and make sure that they go to good loving homes.

You will need

* Coarse wool: white for bear
* Merino tops: beige and lemon for tufting, lemon and orange for wings, lemon for dress and black for the nose and mouth details
* Two 4mm black glass eyes with a single loop
* 10 x 12cm (4 x 4¾in) piece of beige pre-made felt

Tools

* Triangular felting needle, gauge 40
* Foam pad
* Wooden barbecue stick
* Embroidery scissors
* Dressmaking pins
* Waxed dental tape
* Long needle
* Autofade pen
* Fabric glue

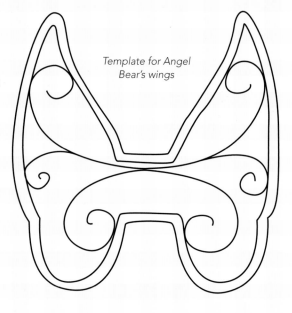

Template for Angel Bear's wings

Instructions

1 Referring to pages 12–17 and using white coarse wool, make the bear's head, nose cone, ears, body, arms and legs. Attach the head to the body. Needle the nose cone to the head and attach the ears and eyes. Needle the nose and mouth details with black Merino wool.

2 Tuft a small area round each eye with lemon Merino wool. Leaving the muzzle, ears, paws and feet as white coarse wool, tuft the rest of bear with beige wool.

3 Joint your bear as shown on pages 26–27.

4 Take two 20cm (8in) lengths of lemon Merino wool, approximately 1.5cm (¾in) thick. Lay one length over each shoulder at the mid point.

5 Cross them over the bear's chest at the front and at the back. Pull them tight and then needle them along the bear's waistline to secure. Leave the long ends trailing to create the skirt of the dress.

6 Add a few more lengths of lemon wool round the bear's waist to hide any gaps and needle to secure them.

7 Wrap a length of orange Merino wool round the waist and needle it smooth to create a belt.

8 Photocopy or trace the wing design and cut it out. Lay it on your piece of pre-made felt and draw round it with the autofade pen. Copy the swirling design onto the felt wings.

9 Place the felt on the foam pad. Using thin lengths of lemon wool, needle a thin border round the edge of the wings.

10 Needle the inner swirling design using thin lengths of lemon wool and then needle the areas in between with orange wool.

11 Cut round the wings, turn them over and trim any fibres that have come through to the other side to neaten them.

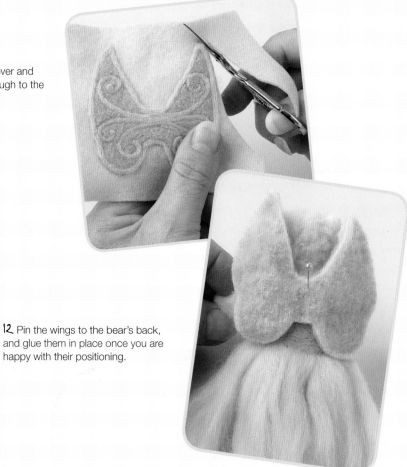

12 Pin the wings to the bear's back, and glue them in place once you are happy with their positioning.

Bride and Groom

Bride

Bella met Henry at the Teddy Bear's Picnic last summer and since then they have been inseparable. She designed her own dress for the occasion: a simple floor length A-line wedding gown decorated with a single flower on the bodice. She is wearing a flowing veil held in place by a floral headdress. Her matching bouquet adds the finishing touch to our blushing bride.

You will need

* Coarse wool: white for bear; ivory for the dress; bright pink, pale pink, white, lemon and green for the flowers
* Merino tops: black and pink for the nose, mouth and rosy cheeks
* Two 4mm black glass eyes with a single loop
* 11 x 15cm (4¼ x 6in) piece of white netting
* White thread

Tools

* Triangular felting needle, gauge 40
* Star felting needle, gauge 38
* Foam pad
* Wooden barbecue stick
* Embroidery scissors
* Large scissors
* Dressmaking pins
* Waxed dental tape
* Long needle
* Sewing needle

Instructions

1 Referring to pages 12–20, use white coarse wool to make the bear's head, nose cone, ears, body, arms and legs with standing feet. Attach the head to the body. Attach the nose cone and ears to the head and sew the eyes in place. Needle the nose and mouth. Needle a few strands of pink wool into each cheek and then attach the legs using the jointing method shown on pages 26–27.

2 For the dress, first layer a 10 x 20cm (4 X 8in) area with ivory wool onto the foam pad. Needle and turn the wool as explained on page 28 until it is slightly larger than the template (see page 62). Lay the template on top of the wool, pin it in place and then cut out the dress shape.

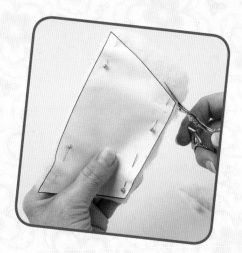

3 Wrap the wool panel round the bear's body. Needle the top 2cm (¾in) of the panel into the bear's body to create the bodice.

4 Slightly overlap the join at the back of the skirt and needle it gently to bind the fibres together. Trim the bottom of the dress to neaten if necessary. Joint the arms using the same technique as for the legs.

Ooh! She's going to look beautiful!

5 For the veil, gather the long edge of an 11 x 15cm (4¼ x 6in) piece of netting and needle it to the top of the bear's head.

6 To make a flower, dampen your hands and roll a few strands of coloured wool in one palm using your index finger. Roll three small balls of bright pink wool and four small balls of pale pink wool for the headdress.

7 Needle a bright pink ball to the top of the bear's head at the front edge of the veil and work to either side with alternate bright pink and pale pink balls to create the headdress. Add a few green fibres between the flowers for the leaves.

8 Needle one small bright pink ball to the front of the dress bodice. Add a few green fibres on either side for leaves.

9 For the bouquet, take a small handful of white coarse wool and needle it into a ball, leaving a few loose fibres at one end. Roll a number of small balls for the flowers using pale pink, bright pink, lemon and white wool, and needle them into the ball to make a bouquet.

10 Needle the loose fibres on the bouquet together to create a bundle of stems, and trim to approximately 1cm (½in). Place the bouquet between the bear's paws and sew it in place to secure.

Template for the wedding dress, half size

Groom

Henry is really looking forward to seeing his bride Bella and to the party afterwards, as there will be lots of honey and cupcakes to eat. For his special day he is wearing a smart waistcoat and top hat. The pink hat band, neck bow and buttonhole match Bella's headdress and bouquet.

You will need

* Coarse wool: light brown for the bear; ivory, bright pink and green for the waistcoat, top hat, buttonhole and neck bow
* Merino tops: black for the nose and mouth
* Two 2mm black glass eyes with a single loop
* Two small white buttons
* White thread

Tools

* Triangular felting needle, gauge 40
* Star felting needle, gauge 38
* Foam pad
* Wooden barbecue stick
* Embroidery scissors
* Large scissors
* Dressmaking pins
* Waxed dental tape
* Long needle
* Sewing needle
* Fabric glue

Instructions

1 Use light brown coarse wool to make the bear's head, nose cone, ears, body, arms and legs with standing feet (see pages 12–20). Attach the head to the body, and the nose cone to the head. Attach the eyes, needle the nose and mouth details and then needle the ears so that they lie slightly low on the head. This is to allow the top hat to sit correctly.

2 Needle a thin line of white wool to outline the waistcoat area.

3 Fill in the waistcoat area with white wool and needle until it is smooth and secure. Joint the bear (see pages 26–27).

4 To create the top hat, first roll a 10cm (4in) length of white wool tightly round a wooden barbecue stick.

5 Slide the stick out and place the cylinder of wool upright on the foam pad. Needle both ends flat.

6 Now lay the cylinder on its side and needle it while turning it. Continue in this way, needling the top, bottom and the sides, until it shrinks to measure approximately 2cm (¾in) high with a diameter of around 18mm (⅝in).

7 To make the brim, lay a 4cm (1½in) diameter circle of white wool on the foam pad. Needle this evenly all over. Turn it over and needle. Continue in this way until the brim shrinks to a circle with a diameter of 2.5cm (1in).

8 Place the cylinder on top of the brim and needle down through the hat to secure the two together.

9 Turn the hat over and needle repeatedly into the middle of the brim to create a concave shape so that the hat can fit onto the bear's round head.

10 Needle a thin band of pink wool round the base of the hat. Glue the hat to the bear's head, then needle it to secure.

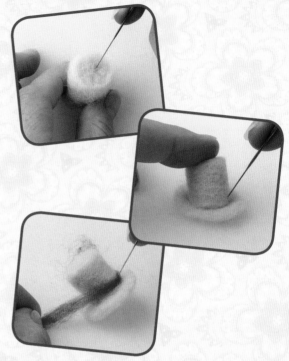

Teddy Tip
When sewing buttons to your bear, take the thread through the bear's body to the back as you sew. Take finishing threads to the back of the bear, trim them and then needle small strands of matching wool to cover any visible stitches or indentations caused by the stitching.

11 Sew two small white buttons down the front of the waistcoat.

12 Needle a small ball of pink wool for the buttonhole flower and add green strands here and there for the leaves.

13 Needle a small flat strip of pink wool. Stab the middle of the strip to shrink it and make a bow shape. Needle it onto your bear to complete his outfit.

Button Bear

It was lovely to rummage through our mum's old button box to find just the right buttons for Bertie Button Bear and his little friend Sadie. They have now taken up residence in the box along with all the coloured buttons and bits and bobs! Sadie loves Bertie's tufted body and conical button hat, which give him a cuddly and quirky look. Bertie loves Sadie's colourful button belt and teeny button nose.

You will need

Bertie Button Bear

* Coarse wool: beige for the bear
* Merino tops: light brown, dark brown and black for tufting, and nose and mouth details
* Two 4mm black glass eyes with a single loop
* 3mm wide purple silk ribbon: 20cm (7¾in) long
* Assorted purple and lilac buttons
* Two small lilac heart buttons
* Lilac thread

Sadie Bear

* Coarse wool: lilac and purple for the bear
* Merino tops: black for the mouth
* Two 2mm black glass eyes with a single loop
* One small pink round button
* Four small heart buttons, assorted colours
* Lilac thread

Tools

* Triangular felting needle, gauge 40
* Foam pad
* Wooden barbecue stick
* Embroidery scissors
* Dressmaking pins
* Waxed dental tape
* Long needle
* Sewing needle
* Glue

My friend Sadie is on page 68

Bertie Button Bear
Instructions

1 Referring to pages 12–17, needle the basic bear parts using beige coarse wool. Attach the head to the body, and the nose cone and eyes to the head. Needle the nose and mouth in black wool and needle the ears slightly low on the side of the head.

2 Referring to page 25, tuft a little dark brown wool round each eye and trim the fibres.

3 Leaving the nose cone, ears, paws and feet untufted, tuft the rest of the head, the arms and the legs with light brown wool and then joint your bear (see pages 26–27).

4 Sew three purple buttons down the chest of the bear.

5 Sew a small lilac heart button to the top of each arm.

6 Create a conical hat by stacking and gluing buttons in descending size order.

7 Glue the button hat to the top of the bear's head at an angle and tie a ribbon bow round the bear's neck.

Sadie Bear
Instructions

1 Referring to pages 12–17 using coarse lilac wool, needle felt the head, ears, body, arms and legs. Needle the nose cone using purple wool. Attach the head to the body, and the ears and nose cone to the head. Needle the mouth details in black Merino wool. Joint your bear (see pages 26–27).

Teddy Tip
To make Sadie smaller than the basic bear, just needle the basic bear parts slightly smaller than the template. See page 96.

2 Lay a thin length of purple wool across each shoulder to create the crossed straps. Needle them in place and then trim the ends to finish at the waist.

3 Needle a 2 x 11cm (¾ x 4¼in) flat purple strip as explained on page 28. Wrap the strip round the bear's waist. Gather it as you needle the upper edge in place.

Rock-a-bye Sadie

Oh that pink piggy nose!

4 Sew a row of small heart-shaped buttons round the waistband. Stitch another heart button where the straps cross, and then sew a tiny button onto Sadie's nose.

Ballet Bear

Bears love to dance. Beatrice is proudly showing off her first grown-up ballet tutu with matching ballet shoes and headband. As Beatrice is a real girly bear, we have decorated her outfit with lovely yellow flowers.

You will need

* Coarse wool: pink and pale pink for the bear; white, pink, yellow and lime green for the tutu, ballet shoes, nose and mouth, headband, flowers and leaves
* Merino tops: white for the ballet shoe ribbons
* Two 4mm black glass eyes with a single loop

Tools

* Triangular felting needle, gauge 40
* Star felting needle, gauge 38
* Foam pad
* Wooden barbecue stick
* Embroidery scissors
* Dressmaking pins
* Waxed dental tape
* Long needle

Instructions

1 Referring to pages 12–17, make the bear's head, body, arms and legs using pink coarse wool. Make the nose cone and ears with pale pink coarse wool. Needle the head to the body, then attach the nose cone and ears to the head. Needle some pink strands into the inner ears and then attach the eyes. Needle the pink mouth and nose.

2 Joint the arms using the jointing method explained on pages 26–27.

3 To create the bodice, wrap the lower two-thirds of the bear's body with white coarse wool and needle it until it is smooth and secure.

4 Needle a few strands of white wool over each shoulder to create the straps.

5 Roll two small balls of yellow wool in the palm of your hand and needle one onto the base of each strap to create the flower decoration. Use a few strands of green wool to needle leaves round the flowers.

6 To create the tutu, first cover a 26 x 6cm (10¼ x 2¼in) area on the foam pad with white coarse wool to a depth of about 1cm (½in). Needle it until it shrinks to approximately 20 x 4cm (8 x 1½in).

7 Cut the panel down the middle to create two long 20 x 2cm (8 x ¾in) strips. Trim to neaten the edges if necessary.

8 Needle one of the strips with yellow spots for the flowers and needle green leaf shapes in between.

9 Place the two strips together with the decorated strip on top and, starting at the back of the bear, needle the long edge of the strips into the bear's waist. Gather the strips as you work. Needle the top of the strips and underneath to get a good secure fixing.

10 Trim the ends of the strips so that they overlap slightly and then gently needle the join at the back of the tutu.

11 Wrap each foot with white coarse wool and needle to secure. Needle a strand of white Merino wool to one side of the ballet shoe. Wrap it round the back of the leg and needle it to the other side to secure. Repeat for the other shoe.

12 Decorate each shoe with a yellow flower and leaves and then join the legs to the body using the jointing technique shown on pages 26–27.

13 Needle a white coarse wool band round the bear's head and then needle yellow flowers and green leaves onto the band.

Disco Bear

Disco Dave loves music and dancing. Every month he hosts a fun event for all his bear friends where he likes to sparkle in his glitzy vest and hat. Metallic fibres are worked into the felting process to create this disco look.

You will need

* Coarse wool: blue for the bear; green, white and grey for the bear's hat, vest and shoes
* Merino tops: black for the sunglasses, nose and mouth
* Sparkly fibres in green and pink
* Silver metallic thread

Tools

* Triangular felting needle, gauge 40
* Star felting needle, gauge 38
* Foam pad
* Wooden barbecue stick
* Embroidery scissors
* Dressmaking pins
* Waxed dental tape
* Long needle
* Sewing needle

Instructions

1 Referring to pages 12–21, use blue coarse wool to make the bear's head, nose cone, one ear, arms with hands and thumbs, and legs with standing feet. Attach the head to the body, and the nose cone and ear to the head. Needle the nose and mouth.

2 Using black Merino wool, needle an oval shape over each eye and a small line between them to create Disco Bear's sunglasses.

3 Using white coarse wool, outline the bear's vest. Fill it in with a thin layer of white wool fibres. Lay sparkly pink fibres on top, then needle another thin layer of white fibres to secure them.

4 Outline the top of the trainers with a thin line of white fibres. Wrap green fibres round one foot, and needle them firmly, shaping the front of the foot so that it is smooth and round. Repeat on the other foot.

5 Sew the laces on using metallic thread, starting and finishing on the underside of the foot. Glue the ends to secure.

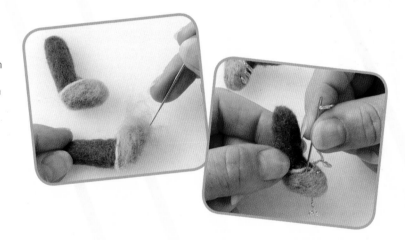

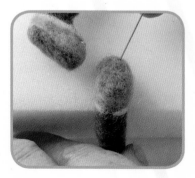

6 For the sole, needle an oval of grey wool fibres onto the bottom of the shoe, covering the ends of the laces.

7 Joint the arms and legs, following the instructions on pages 26–27.

8 To make the hat, needle a fairly firm ball of white coarse wool, approximately 3.5cm (1¼in) in diameter. Needle one side of the ball flat to create the dome shape of the hat, so it will fit comfortably on the bear's head.

9 Turn the dome over and needle the underside to create a concave shape.

10 Lay a few sparkly green fibres and then some green wool fibres over the cap. Needle them to secure.

11 To add detail, needle a criss-cross of thin lines of green wool fibres onto the hat and a small ball in the centre.

12 For the brim, needle a small flat semicircle leaving loose fibres along the straight edge. Needle the peak to the hat and then needle the hat to the bear's head.

Arty Bear

Vincent van Bear is creating chaos again! He is bearly recognisable in his studio under all those splodges of paint. With his Dali moustache and his denim, paint-splattered dungarees, he is all ready to get started on his next teddy portrait.

You will need

* Coarse wool: bright pink and pale pink for the bear; blue, red, orange, green, black and light brown for the dungarees, beret and palette
* Merino tops: black for the nose and moustache
* Two 2mm black glass eyes with a single loop
* Two small blue buttons
* PVA glue
* Wooden barbecue stick
* Thin silver-coloured wire
* Black felt-tip pen

Tools

* Triangular felting needle, gauge 40
* Star felting needle, gauge 38
* Foam pad
* Wooden barbecue stick
* Embroidery scissors
* Dressmaking pins
* Waxed dental tape
* Long needle

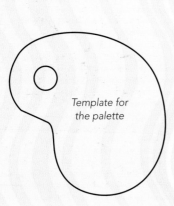

Template for the palette

Instructions

1 Referring to pages 12–21, needle the basic bear's head, body and one ear using bright pink coarse wool. Make two legs with standing feet and two arms with thumbed hands. Make the nose cone using pale pink wool.

2 Needle the head to the body. Attach the pale pink nose cone and one ear.

3 Attach the eyes and needle the nose in black Merino wool. To make the moustache, pull a thin 4.5cm (1¾in) length of black Merino wool and needle the centre of it just under the bear's nose.

4 Smear the ends of the moustache with a little PVA glue, bending them up slightly and leave to dry.

5 Wrap and then needle the lower half of the body with blue coarse wool.

6 Outline the bib area of the dungarees with strands of blue wool and then fill it in.

7 Needle the straps and sew a button to the base of each strap.

8 Wrap the legs from the top to the ankles with blue coarse wool. Needle until firm and secure.

9 To create the flared trouser leg, first lay a 5 x 12cm (2 x 4¾in) panel of blue wool on your foam pad and needle it flat (see page 28). Needle a little wool along one long edge.

10 Wrap the felt round the ankle with the thicker edge at the bottom and then needle it onto the leg.

11 Attach the arms and legs using the jointing technique explained on pages 26–27.

12 To create the beret, lay a 6cm (2¼in) diameter circle of black wool onto your foam pad. Needle it all over, pushing your needle at a shallow angle from the edge towards the centre until it shrinks to half the size.

13 Place the beret on the bear's head on the side without the ear and needle round the edge of the beret, tucking the fibres under to create a neat edge as you work.

14 Needle small splodges of coloured wool randomly over the bear's dungarees to represent paint splashes and then needle the palette to the bear's hand.

15 For the palette, lay a 9cm (3½in) wide oval area of light brown coarse wool onto your foam pad. Needle it, turning it over frequently until it shrinks in size to measure approximately 4.5cm (1¾in) across.

16 Pin the template on top of the felted panel. Trim round it with scissors and then needle the edge to neaten.

17 Cut the thumb hole with embroidery scissors to the width of the bear's thumb and needle round it to neaten. Needle a few splodges of coloured wool onto the palette.

The paintbrush

1 Cut off the pointed end of the barbecue stick so that it measures 5cm (2in) long and colour it black with a felt-tip pen.

2 When dry, glue some orange fibres round the blunt end of the stick, then wrap it with wire.

3 Smear the end of the fibres with a little watered-down PVA glue and press them together to create the pointed brush end. Glue the brush to the bear's paw.

Santa Paws

Every year Santa Paws visits the bears with his sack of toys and brings them presents. He is too fat to go down the chimney, so instead he joins in the Christmas festivities with a jug of mead and a honey cupcake. He is round and jolly, so more wool is added to the basic bear's body to give him his characteristic shape. White eyebrows and a traditional red wool suit and hat edged with white complete the festive look.

You will need

* Coarse wool: light yellow for the bear; white, red and black for the eyebrows, suit, hat and boots
* Merino tops: black for the nose and mouth
* Two 4mm black glass eyes with a single loop

The sack and toys

* Beige 4-ply (fingering) yarn for the sack
* Knitting needles, 2.5mm (US size 1)
* Coarse wool: mid yellow, orange, jade, light brown, red and white for the toys
* Two 2mm black glass eyes with a single loop
* Merino tops: black for the gingerbread man's features and red for the candy cane
* Metallic thread
* Florist's wire and tape for the candy cane

Tools

* Triangular felting needle, gauge 40
* Star felting needle, gauge 38
* Foam pad
* Wooden barbecue stick
* Dressmaking pins
* Embroidery scissors
* Waxed dental tape
* Long needle
* Fabric glue

Instructions

1 Referring to pages 12–17, using light yellow coarse wool, first make the bear's head, nose cone, one ear, body and arms. Add a little extra wool to the body to make Santa Paws chubby. Attach the head to the body, then attach the nose cone and ear. Add the eyes and features, and gently needle white wool eyebrows above the eyes, so that they remain fluffy.

2 Wrap each arm down to the wrist with red coarse wool. Add a strip of white wool round each wrist, needling it gently so it remains fluffy.

3 Referring to pages 20–21, needle two legs with standing feet using red coarse wool. Cover the feet with black coarse wool to create the boots. Wrap a strip of white coarse wool round the top of each boot, needling it gently so it remains fluffy.

4 Cover the body with red coarse wool, giving the bear's tunic a V-neck. Needle a length of white wool round the bear's hips, and a border round the neck edge and down the front of the bear's tunic.

5 Joint the bear, referring to pages 26–27.

6 Using the template below as a guide to make the hat, loosely needle a cone using red coarse wool.

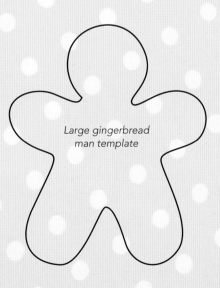

Small gingerbread man template

Large gingerbread man template

Template for hat

7 Place the hat on the side of the bear's head without the ear and needle round the edge to secure it.

8 Needle a band of white coarse wool round the bottom of the hat.

9 Fold the top of the hat down. Lift it slightly, then needle a line on along the inner fold. This will secure the fold.

10 Needle over the surface of the hat so that it shrinks to the shape of the bear's head.

11 Make a small white bobble by rolling a tiny piece of white wool in the palm of your hand, then needle it so it retains its bobble shape. Glue it to the end of the hat. Secure the bobble with a felting needle, while the glue dries.

Santa Paws' sack

Sack

Cast on 20 stitches.
Knit 50 rows.
Cast off.
Fold the knitted strip in half and then sew the sides to create the sack.

Toy bear

To make the toy bear, follow the instructions for the basic bear on pages 12–19 using the tiny bear template on page 96.

Orange

Make a small orange ball by rolling a little piece of orange wool in your palm, then needle it all round firmly so it retains its round shape. Needle a few black Merino fibres into the top.

Parcel

The parcel is approximately 2.5cm (1in) long, 1cm (½in) wide and 1cm (½in) deep. Make a loose oval and needle the ends to flatten them, then needle the four sides to create the rectangular shape. Tie a small length of metallic thread round the parcel and finish it with a bow.

Gingerbread Man

Needle a firm flat panel of light brown wool measuring 7 x 8cm (2¾ x 3¼in) (see page 28). Photocopy and cut out the large gingerbread man template (see page 83). Pin it to the panel and cut it out. Lay the gingerbread man on your foam pad, needle it shallowly across the surface, working from the edges towards the centre at all times. Move the shape round as you work until it has shrunk to the size of the smaller template. Trim the outer shape to neaten if necessary. Needle the eyes and mouth using black and red Merino tops.

Candy cane

Cut a 4cm (1½in) length of florist's wire, bend the top over and wrap the wire with florist's tape. Wrap white coarse wool round the wire and lightly needle it to secure. Take a narrow length of red Merino wool and spiral it round the candy cane. Needle to secure.

Burlesque Bear

Our merry band of bears would not be complete without the amazing Brenda, our all singing and dancing Burlesque Bear. She beguiles audiences with her husky voice and her bejewelled costume and likes nothing better than entertaining her teddy friends.

You will need

* Coarse wool: pale pink for bear; dark red and black for dress, hat, gloves and stockings
* Merino tops: bright pink, mid pink, turquoise and black for the nose and mouth, rosy cheeks, eye shadow and lashes, dress decoration and hair
* Two 4mm black glass eyes with a single loop
* Two red flower gems
* Small round red faceted gems

Tools

* Triangular felting needle, gauge 40
* Star felting needle, gauge 38
* Foam pad
* Wooden barbecue stick
* Embroidery scissors
* Dressmaking scissors
* Waxed dental tape
* Long needle
* Fabric glue

Instructions

1 Referring to pages 12–17, use pale pink coarse wool to make your bear's head, nose cone, ears, body, arms and legs. Attach the head to the body, and attach the nose cone and ears to the head.

2 Attach the eyes, needle the nose and mouth details in bright pink Merino wool and then needle a few strands of turquoise wool above each eye for eye shadow.

3 To create the rosy cheeks, needle a few strands of mid pink wool to each side of the nose cone.

4 Needle a few fibres of black Merino wool to the edge of each eye and trim them to create the eyelashes.

5 For the costume, needle the centre of an 8cm (3¼in), thin length of dark red wool to the middle of the bear's chest. Wrap and then needle the trailing ends round the bear to the back to create the top edge of the costume. Trim the ends to neaten.

6 Wrap the lower two-thirds of the body below the edging in dark red coarse wool and needle it until smooth. Create two small balls of dark red wool on the foam pad and then needle them onto the chest to create the bust.

7 Decorate the bodice by needling thin bands of bright pink Merino wool above and below the bust. Add a halter-neck strap.

8 For the skirt, lay a 4 x 20cm (1½ x 7¾in) strip of dark red coarse wool on the foam pad and needle it until it shrinks (see page 28). Cut out a rectangle measuring 2 x 14cm (¾ x 5½in).

9 Starting at the front of the bear, needle the centre of the long edge of the strip to the bear's tummy. Needle the two ends of the strip all the way round the bear so they meet at the back.

10 If necessary, trim the ends of the strips to fit together and then gently needle them in place.

11 Needle a thin border of bright pink Merino wool round the bear's hips, along the top of the skirt.

12 Make the stockings by wrapping and then needling each leg with black coarse wool to 1cm (½in) from the top. To create the gloves, wrap and then needle the lower arms and paws with black wool and then needle a border of bright pink wool around the edge of the gloves.

13 Joint the bear following the instructions on pages 26–27.

14 The top hat is made by first rolling a small, tight sausage of black coarse wool, 2cm (¾in) thick and 3cm (1¼in) long. Needle this until it is firm and has reduced in size to measure 1cm (½in) thick and 1.5cm (⅝in) long.

15 Lay a 3cm (1¼in) diameter loose ball of black coarse wool on your foam pad for the brim and needle it flat until it shrinks to 2cm (¾in).

16 Needle the top of the hat to the brim and then needle the hat onto the bear's head.

17 Needle a loose swirl of bright pink Merino wool to the head for the hair. Needle a small feather into the hair.

18 Wrap the neck with a few strands of black Merino wool and needle to create a choker necklace.

19 Glue one of the flower gems to the middle of the necklace and the other to the centre of the pink band around the bear's hips. Glue red faceted gems onto the costume for extra sparkle.

Baby Bears

Baby bears are fun and quick to make, but remember, when working this small, be careful not to prick your fingers! The instructions for making the cookies are on page 92.

You will need

* Coarse wool: pale yellow for the bear; white for the nappy and bootees
* Merino tops: yellow, pink and black for the hair, cheeks and nose and mouth details
* Two 2mm black glass eyes with a single loop
* Yellow embroidery thread
* Small plastic safety pin embellishment

Tools

* Triangular felting needle, gauge 40
* Star felting needle, gauge 38
* Foam pad
* Embroidery scissors
* Waxed dental floss
* Long needle
* Wooden barbecue stick
* Fabric glue
* Dressmaking pins

Template for nappy

Instructions

1 Use the baby bear template (page 96) to help you with the amounts of coarse wool needed for your mini bear. Make your body parts using pale yellow wool. See pages 12–17.

2 Needle the head to the body, then attach the nose cone, the ears and eyes to the head and needle the tiny nose and mouth details using black merino wool.

3 Needle a few strands of pink Merino wool to each cheek and a tuft of yellow Merino wool to the top of the head.

4 Wrap each foot in white wool, needling it into each foot to secure the fibres and create the bootees.

5 Joint your bear following the instructions on pages 26–27.

6 To create the nappy, refer to page 28 and layer a 14 x 8cm (5½ x 3¼in) triangle shape on your foam pad with white wool. Needle it until it has shrunk to slightly larger than the template.

7 Using the template opposite, pin the shape to the wool. Trim the wool with scissors to neaten.

8 Lay the triangle of felt down with the long edge at the top. Lay the teddy, face up, on top. Pull the middle point up through the bear's legs and needle it a few times into the bear's tummy to secure the nappy.

9 Wrap the two long ends round to the front of the bear so they meet in the middle. Needle felt the ends to secure.

10 Joint the arms to your bear using the same jointing technique as for the legs.

11 Glue a small embroidery thread bow to each bootee and the mini safety pin to the nappy.

Teddy Bear's Picnic

Now our merry band of bears is complete, it's time for some fun. They are going to have their first teddy bear's picnic in their very own fluffy forest and will need wee woolly goodies to eat. On these two pages we have provided you with recipes for scrummy gateaux, cupcakes (a teddy's favourite), cookies and breads.

Tools

For all the picnic projects you will need:

* Triangular felting needle, gauge 40
* Star felting needle, gauge 38
* Foam pad
* Wooden barbecue stick
* Embroidery scissors
* Scalpel

Gateaux
You will need

* Coarse wool: beige for the cake base
* Merino tops: pink white and red

1 Take a 20cm (7¾in) strip of beige wool, approximately 3cm (1¼in) wide. Roll this into a loose sausage. Lay it down on your foam pad and needle the centre a few times to secure the sausage shape.

2 Now hold the sausage upright on your pad and needle one end of it flat. The sausage shape will become fatter as you needle. Turn it over and repeat on the other end until you have created a rough cylinder shape.

3 Lay it on its side and needle round the shape to neaten the cylinder.

4 Repeat, working on the ends and round the middle until you have a cake base shape with a 3cm (1¼in) diameter, 2cm (¾in) deep.

5 Needle a little band of pink wool round the middle of the cake for the filling and then needle a thin layer of pink wool over the top of the cake for the icing.

6 Needle a small ball of white wool to the middle of the top of the cake and add a small ball of red on top.

7 Needle small balls of red wool round the edge of the top of the cake.

For our chocolate-loving bears, use dark brown wool for the filling and the icing on this yummy gateau.

To make a variety of gateaux for the picnic, use different coloured wools for the icing and make the cake base cylinder shape larger and flatter or deeper.

Cookies
You will need

* Course wool: beige
* Merino tops: red

1 Take a small clump of beige wool. Shape it into a ball and then needle it all over until it becomes a flat disc shape measuring approximately 2cm (¾in) in diameter.

2 Needle a small ball of red wool to the top for the cherry.

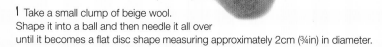

Cupcakes
You will need

* Coarse wool: blue
* Merino tops: pink, cream and red

1 Take a 10cm (4in) strip of blue wool approximately 2cm (¾in) wide, roll it into a sausage and needle it into a small cylinder shape. Use steps 2 to 4 of the gateaux to help you.

2 Create the typical cupcake case shape by needling one end of the cylinder while turning it, until it tapers slightly.

3 To create a base for the swirly icing, first needle a pea-sized ball of cream wool onto the top of the blue cake case.

4 Take two 10cm (4in) lengths of wool – one pink and one beige. Lay them side by side at the edge of the blue cake case and needle the ends to secure. Now wrap the length of wool round and round, needling it as you wrap to create the swirl of icing.

5 When you reach the top, trim back any excess wool fibres and needle the ends to neaten.

6 Needle a small ball of red wool to the top for the cherry.

Our teddies love cupcakes. Make different colours and sizes to suit all our different shaped bears!

Breads
You will need

* Course wool: beige
* Merino tops: light brown

Bread roll

1 Use a small clump of beige wool to create a slightly flattened ball shape approximately 2cm (¾in) in diameter.

2 Needle a few fibres of light brown wool over the top of the ball.

Cottage loaf

1 Needle a slightly flattened ball of beige wool so that it measures approximately 3cm (1¼in) in diameter.

2 Needle a smaller flattened ball. Place the smaller ball on top of the large one and needle through the two balls to bind them together.

3 Needle a few strands of light brown wool over the smaller ball to add interest.

4 Needle repeatedly into the middle of the top of the loaf to create an indentation.

French loaf

1 Needle a 6cm (2¼in) long firm sausage using beige wool.

2 Lay some light brown fibres across the top of the sausage and needle until smooth.

3 Using a scalpel, cut four V-shaped slots along the top of the loaf. Remove the small V-sections.

Templates

The templates below are all reproduced actual size.

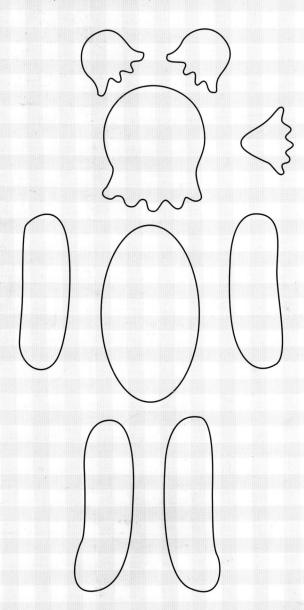

Basic bear template

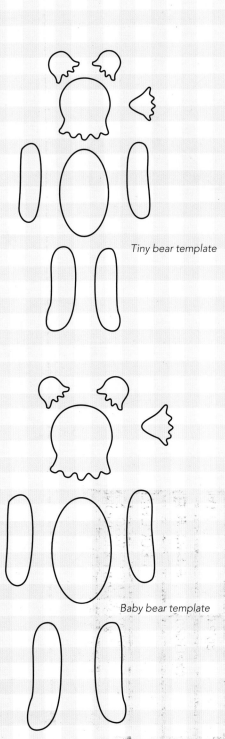

Tiny bear template

Baby bear template